IRAQ

EXPLORE THE COUNTRIES

Big Buddy Books
An Imprint of Abdo Publishing
abdopublishing.com

Julie Murray

abdopublishing.com

Published by Abdo Publishing, a division of ABDO, PO Box 398166, Minneapolis, Minnesota 55439.
Copyright © 2016 by Abdo Consulting Group, Inc. International copyrights reserved in all countries. No part
of this book may be reproduced in any form without written permission from the publisher. Big Buddy Books™
is a trademark and logo of Abdo Publishing.

Printed in the United States of America, North Mankato, Minnesota.
092015
012016

THIS BOOK CONTAINS
RECYCLED MATERIALS

Cover Photo: STR/AFP/Getty Images.
Interior Photos: Anadolu Agency/Getty Images (p. 19); SABAH ARAR/AFP/Getty Images (pp. 35, 37);
    ASSOCIATED PRESS (pp. 19, 29); DEA/ARCHIVIO J. LANGE/GETTY IMAGES (p. 11); DEA/G.
    DAGLI ORTI/Getty Images (p. 16); DEA/C. SAPPA/Getty Images (p. 21); Evening Standard/Getty Images
    (p. 15); Heritage Images/Glow Images (p. 31); © iStockphoto.com (pp. 5, 25, 34, 35); Juniors/Glow
    Images (p. 23); Stephen Lovekin/Getty Images (p. 33); OLIVIER MORIN/AFP/Getty Images (p. 17);
    Francoise De Mulder/Getty Images (p. 17); KHALIL AL-MURSHIDI/AFP/Getty Images (p. 9); Pierre
    PERRIN/Getty Images (p. 15); Print Collector/Getty Images (p. 13); AHMAD AL-RUBAYE/AFP/Getty
    Images (pp. 9, 27); ALI AL-SAADI/AFP/Getty Images (p. 34); AZHAR SHALLAL/AFP/Getty Images
    (p. 35); Shutterstock.com (pp. 11, 19, 38), wollertz/Deposit Photos (p. 38).

Coordinating Series Editor: Megan M. Gunderson
Editor: Katie Lajiness
Contributing Editor: Marcia Zappa
Graphic Design: Adam Craven

Country population and area figures taken from the CIA World Factbook.

Library of Congress Cataloging-in-Publication Data

Murray, Julie, 1969-
 Iraq / Julie Murray.
    pages cm. -- (Explore the countries)
 Includes index.
 ISBN 978-1-68078-068-0
 1. Iraq--Juvenile literature. I. Title.
 DS70.62.M87 2016
 956.7--dc23
                    2015025167

IRAQ

CONTENTS

AROUND THE WORLD

SAY IT

Iraq
ih-RAHK

Our world has many countries. Each country has beautiful land. It has its own rich history. And, the people have their own languages and ways of life.

Iraq is a country in Asia. What do you know about Iraq? Let's learn more about this place and its story!

Did You Know?

Arabic and Kurdish are official languages in Iraq. Turkmen and Assyrian are also official in some areas of the country.

Deserts cover almost two-fifths of Iraq's land. These are found mostly in the southern and western parts of the country.

5

Passport to Iraq

Iraq is located in a part of the world known as the Middle East. Iraq shares borders with six countries. It also borders the Persian Gulf.

Iraq's total area is 169,235 square miles (438,317 sq km). More than 37 million people live there.

WHERE IN THE WORLD?

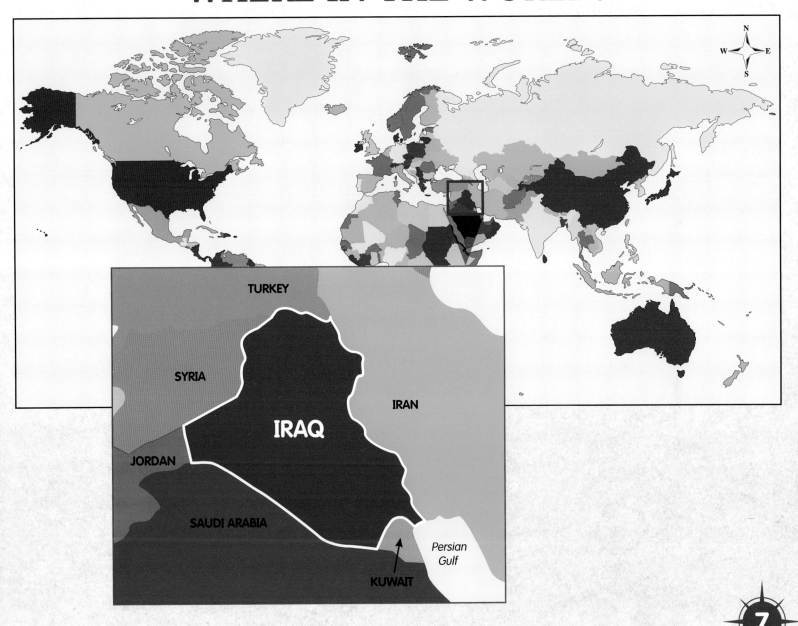

IMPORTANT CITIES

Baghdad is Iraq's **capital** and largest city, with about 6.6 million people. Founded in 762, the city has long been an important **cultural** center in the Middle East.

Today, this very old city has become quite modern. People in Baghdad enjoy spending time in the city's gardens and public parks. With a growing population, **suburbs** spread out in all directions.

SAY IT

Baghdad
BAG-dad

mosque
MAHSK

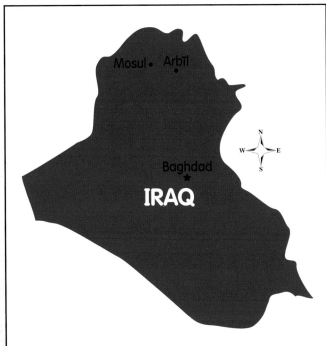

Al-Zawra Park in Baghdad holds a flower festival every year. Many families love to walk through the park to see the flowers.

A mosque is a Muslim place of worship. Umm al-Qura is one of the largest mosques in Baghdad. There are eight minarets that surround the mosque. These towers are used to announce prayer five times a day.

Mosul is Iraq's second-largest city, with about 1.7 million people. The city is home to the al-Hadba minaret. This minaret dates back to 1172. Mosul has increased trade. And, the city is now a center of cloth and farming businesses, among others.

About 50 miles (80 km) east of Mosul is Iraq's third-largest city, Arbīl. About 1.2 million people live there. It is one of the oldest continuously lived-in towns in the world. It has long been home to many of the area's **Christians**. Today, Arbīl is known for farming.

SAY IT

Mosul
MOH-sul

Arbīl
uhr-BEEL

Mosul is on the Tigris River. Five bridges connect different parts of the city across the river.

Arbīl is known for growing sesame (*left*), corn, and fruit.

IRAQ IN HISTORY

One of the world's earliest **cultures** began between the Tigris and the Euphrates Rivers. This area was known as Mesopotamia.

Around 1750 BC, Babylon became one of the largest cities in Mesopotamia. There, many different kinds of people lived and worked together to form a great society.

The **Arabs** took over Mesopotamia during the AD 600s. They brought **Islam** to the area and slowly changed the people's belief system.

Did You Know?

Arabs were the first people to call the country Iraq. The name means "the fertile land."

Babylonians created early forms of math and writing.

The **Ottoman Empire** took over the area during the 1500s. It ruled for more than 400 years.

The Ottomans were in charge of Iraq until **World War I**. Then Britain set up a monarchy in Iraq. A monarchy is a country run by a king or queen. The monarchy lasted from 1921 to 1958.

After this, there was much unrest in Iraq. The country fought Iran over land in the 1980s. And, it attacked Kuwait in 1990. This led to the Persian Gulf War, which Iraq lost in 1991.

In 2003, the United States went to war with Iraq. This led to the capture of government leader Saddam Hussein. The war ended in 2011.

Saddam Hussein was Iraq's leader from 1979 to 2003.

From 1916 to 1918, King Faisal helped destroy the Ottoman Empire during World War I.

SAY IT

Saddam Hussein
sah-DAHM hoo-SAYN

Faisal
FAY-sihl

TIMELINE

About 750

Baghdad was the center of trade and **culture**. It grew into a city of more than 1 million people.

1534

The **Ottoman Empire** ruled Mesopotamia. It was one of the most powerful empires in the world. Mesopotamia included most of Iraq and parts of nearby countries.

1927

The first oil field meant to make money was started in northern Iraq. Oil became a large part of the country's **economy**.

1932

Free from British control, Iraq became an independent area. And, the country joined the League of Nations. This group was formed to keep peace between countries.

1980–1988

Iraq and Iran fought over land, politics, and faith. At least 1 million people were hurt or killed.

2012

Eight athletes from Iraq went to the Summer Olympics in London, England. This was the country's 13th appearance since Iraq first joined the games in 1948.

An Important Symbol

Iraq's flag has three stripes. They are red, white, and black. The green **Arabic** writing in the middle reads "God is great."

Iraq is a **parliamentary democracy**. The prime minister is the head of government. The president is the head of state.

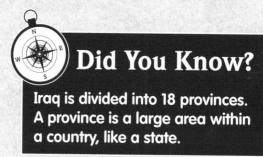

Did You Know?

Iraq is divided into 18 provinces. A province is a large area within a country, like a state.

SAY IT

Fuad Masum
fyoo-AD MA-suhm

Haidar al-Abadi
HAY-der AL-a-BA-dee

Iraq's most recent flag was approved in 2008.

Fuad Masum was elected president of Iraq in 2014.

Haidar al-Abadi became Iraq's prime minister in 2014.

ACROSS THE LAND

Iraq is more than just a desert. It has mountains, plains, and wet areas. Rainy days are uncommon in Iraq. So, Iraq's farming needs river water. The country's major rivers include the Tigris and the Euphrates.

Did You Know?

In the summer, the average temperature in Iraq's lowlands is 95°F (35°C). In the winter, the temperature is 35°F (2°C) to 60°F (16°C).

The Tigris River is about 1,180 miles (1,900 km) long. In southern Iraq, it meets the Euphrates River before flowing into the Persian Gulf.

The riverbanks in Iraq are rich with plant and animal life. Willows, poplars, and licorice plants grow along the riverbanks. Iraq's rivers, streams, and lakes are full of fish. These include carp, catfish, and loach.

Iraq is home to many kinds of animals. Wolves, foxes, and wild pigs live near bodies of water. The **Arabian** sand gazelle lives in the desert. These areas are also home to lizards and snakes.

Arabian sand gazelles eat leaves and grass. They get water through the plants they eat.

23

EARNING A LIVING

Iraq produces a lot of important goods. Many people work in the oil business. Factories make goods such as cement, soap, and foods.

Iraq's main crops are wheat, barley, rice, and dates. Many people raise livestock for milk and meat.

A small number of Iraqi women work outside of the house. But most take care of their families and homes.

Iraq is one of the top ten oil producers in the world. Most of the country's oil fields are in the south.

Did You Know?

Few people in Iraq are farmers because the land is too dry.

25

LIFE IN IRAQ

Iraq has a rich **cultural** history. Different types of people were taken in by Iraq when it separated from the **Ottoman Empire**. These groups brought their own foods, arts, and hobbies.

Most Iraqi meals are served with rice and flatbread. Chicken and lamb are popular meats. Dips, such as hummus and baba ghanoush, are common before meals.

Like many Middle Eastern countries, soccer is the favorite sport in Iraq. Millions of people watch soccer on television.

Many Iraqis watch live soccer at the People's Stadium in Baghdad.

27

The arts are plentiful in Iraq. Works of art include paintings, jewelry, and dishes. Dance, theater, and poems add to Iraq's current creative style.

Most people in Iraq are **Muslim**. The two major **Islamic** groups are Shia and Sunni. More than half of the people are Shia.

 Did You Know?

In Iraq, children must attend school from ages 6 to 12. Secondary schools are open to students across the country.

Around 500 students study the arts at Baghdad School of Music and Ballet.

FAMOUS FACES

Many powerful people are from Iraq. Nebuchadrezzar II was king of Babylonia. This was the large area around the **capital** city of Babylon. He was born around 630 BC. He ruled from 605 to 561 BC. His kingdom covered most of the Middle East.

Nebuchadrezzar II was known for taking over cities and claiming them as his own. He overcame Jerusalem in 597 BC. He is well-known for the **legendary** hanging gardens of Babylon. The gardens are one of the seven wonders of the ancient world.

SAY IT

Nebuchadrezzar
neh-byuh-kuh-DREH-zuhr

According to legend, Nebuchadrezzar II created the hanging gardens of Babylon for his wife. She missed the hills and valleys where she grew up.

Zainab Salbi is an Iraqi-American. She is known for her work helping others. Salbi was born in September 1969, in Baghdad. Her father flew planes for Saddam Hussein. She moved to the United States at age 19.

The Iran-Iraq War made Salbi want to help women hurt by war. She started a group to help women in Iraq and other countries. This group helps women learn job skills and start their own businesses.

SAY IT

Zainab Salbi
ZAY-nuhb SAL-bee

Salbi's group, Women for Women International, has given women more than $100 million.

TOUR BOOK

Imagine traveling to Iraq! Here are some places you could go and things you could do.

 ## Visit

Walk through the Gate of Ishtar in Babylon. This city was once the **capital** of Mesopotamia. Built around 575 BC, the gate is covered with pictures of dragons and bulls.

 ## See

Visit one of the largest zoos in the Middle East! The Baghdad Zoo is a 200-acre (80-ha) park with more than 1,000 animals.

 Explore

The Ur of the Chaldees is a Mesopotamian city said to be where Abraham was born. He is an important person in many beliefs. The Ur dates back to 4000 BC.

Learn

The National Museum of Iraq reopened in 2015 after being closed for 12 years. It contains prized pieces from Mesopotamian society.

Swim

Lake Habbaniyah is in the desert outside of Baghdad. It holds floodwater from the Euphrates River. Many people swim and play on the beach.

A GREAT COUNTRY

The story of Iraq is important to our world. Iraq is a land of huge deserts and plentiful riverbanks. It is a country of strong people who have a rich history.

The people and places that make up Iraq offer something special. They help make the world a more beautiful, interesting place.

In Baghdad, Al-Zawra Park's Ferris wheel is more than 180 feet (55 m) tall! It is the second highest in the Middle East.

Iraq Up Close

Official Name: Republic of Iraq

Flag:

Population (rank): 37,056,169
(July 2015 est.)
(40th most-populated country)

Total Area (rank): 169,235 square miles
(59th largest country)

Capital: Baghdad

Official Languages: Arabic, Kurdish, Turkmen, Assyrian

Currency:
Iraqi dinar

Form of Government:
Parliamentary democracy

National Anthem:
"Mawtini" (My Homeland)

Important Words

Arab of or relating to a member of the people who are originally from the Arabian Peninsula and who now live mostly in the Middle East and northern Africa. Something Arabian relates to Arab people or culture or the Arabic language.

capital a city where government leaders meet.

Christian (KRIHS-chuhn) a person who practices Christianity, which is a religion that follows the teachings of Jesus Christ.

culture (KUHL-chuhr) the arts, beliefs, and ways of life of a group of people.

economy the way that a country produces, sells, and buys goods and services.

Islam a religion based on a belief in Allah as God and Muhammad as his prophet.

legendary of or relating to a legend, which is an old story that many believe, but cannot be proven true.

Muslim a person who practices Islam.

Ottoman Empire an empire created by Turkish tribes in Asia that grew to be one of the most powerful states in the world during the 1400s and 1500s.

parliamentary democracy a government in which the power is held by the people, who exercise it by voting. It is run by a cabinet whose members belong to the legislature.

suburb a town, village, or community just outside a city.

World War I a war fought in Europe from 1914 to 1918.

Websites

To learn more about Explore the Countries, visit **booklinks.abdopublishing.com**. These links are routinely monitored and updated to provide the most current information available.

INDEX